VINTAGE

EMBLEMS

LOGO DESIGN

SYMBOLS

INSPIRATION COMPENDIUM

AN IMAGE ARCHIVE FOR
ARTISTS and DESIGNERS

EDITIONS Vault

VINTAGE LOGO DESIGN INSPIRATION

INTRODUCTION

This pictorial archive from Vault Editions is a treasury of 540 engravings, etchings and woodblock prints documenting European and British emblems, symbols, insignias, heraldry, and coats arms of the 19th, 18th and 17th-century. Expect to find epic imagery of masonic and odd fellows symbols, snakes, skulls, swords, eagles, devils, memento mori, dragons, serpents, hourglasses, anchors, globes, hammers, hands, lions, crosses, banners, borders and much more.

VINTAGE LOGO DESIGN INSPIRATION

VAULT EDITIONS

FEATURES

This book comes with a unique download link providing instant access to high-resolution files of all images featured. These images can be used in art and graphic design projects or printed and framed to make stunning decorative artworks.

DOWNLOAD YOUR FILES

Downloading your files is simple. To access your digital files, please go to the last page of this book and follow the instructions.

For technical assistance, please email:
info@vaulteditions.com

Bibliographical Note

This book is a new work created by Vault Editions Ltd.

ISBN: 978-1-925968-58-3

454

455

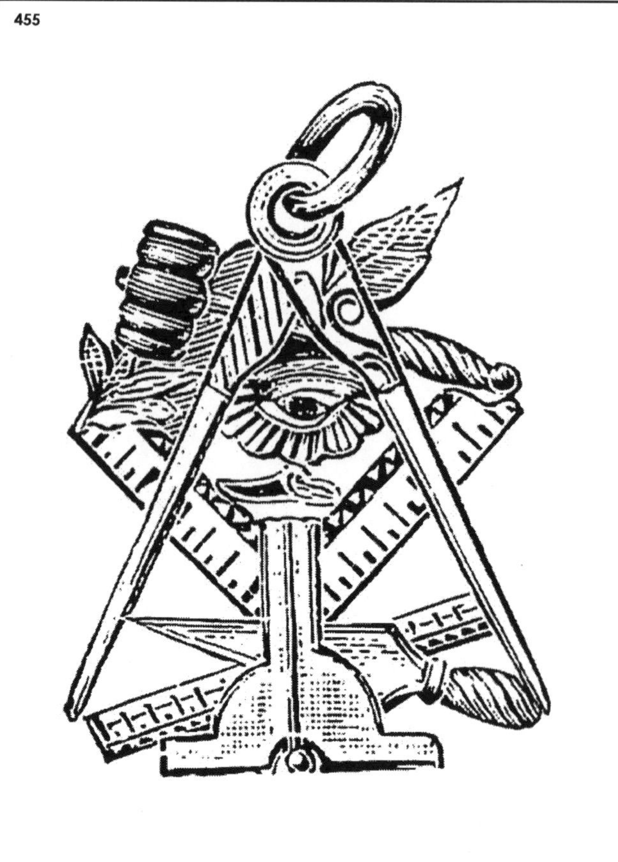

456

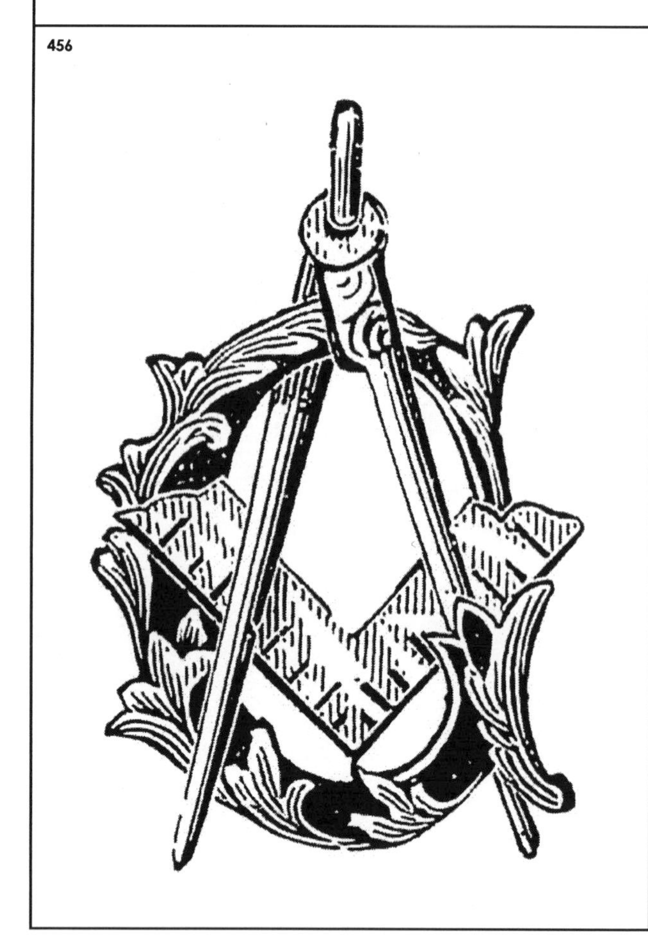

457

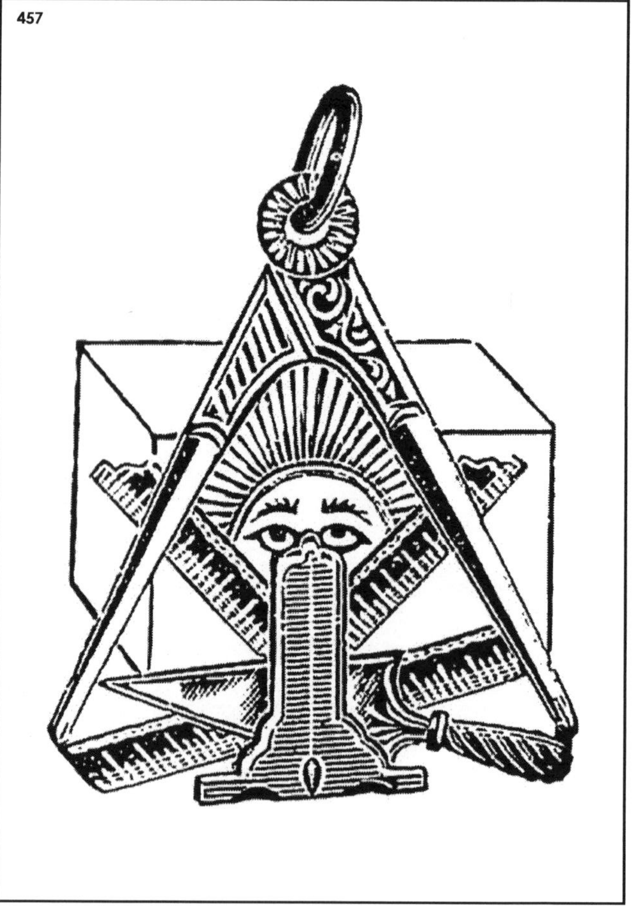

458

459

460

461

462

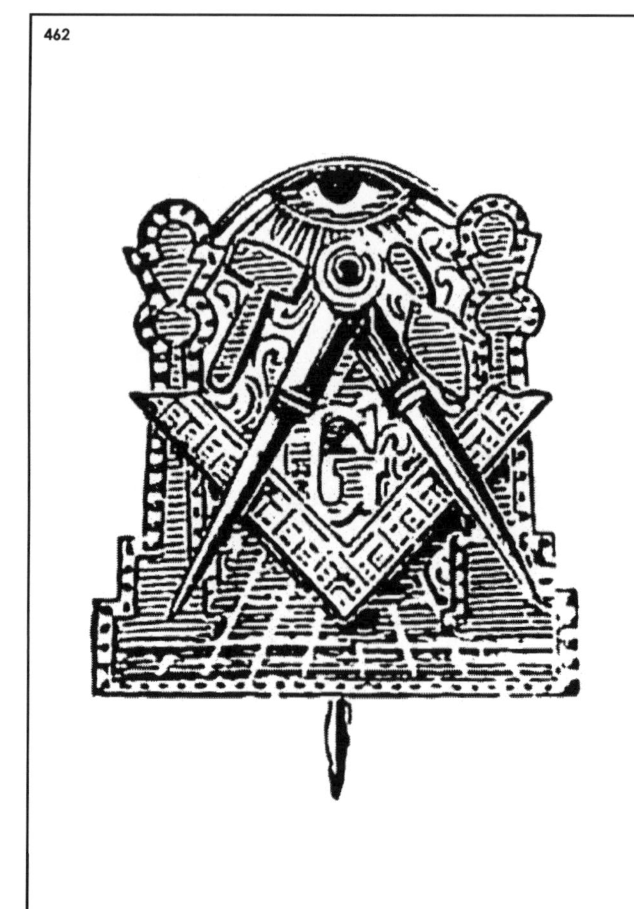

463

464

465

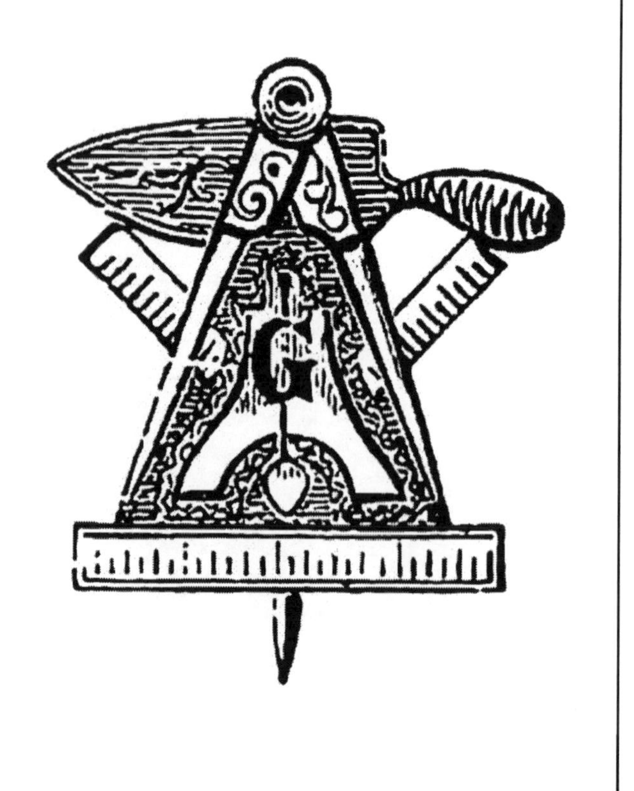

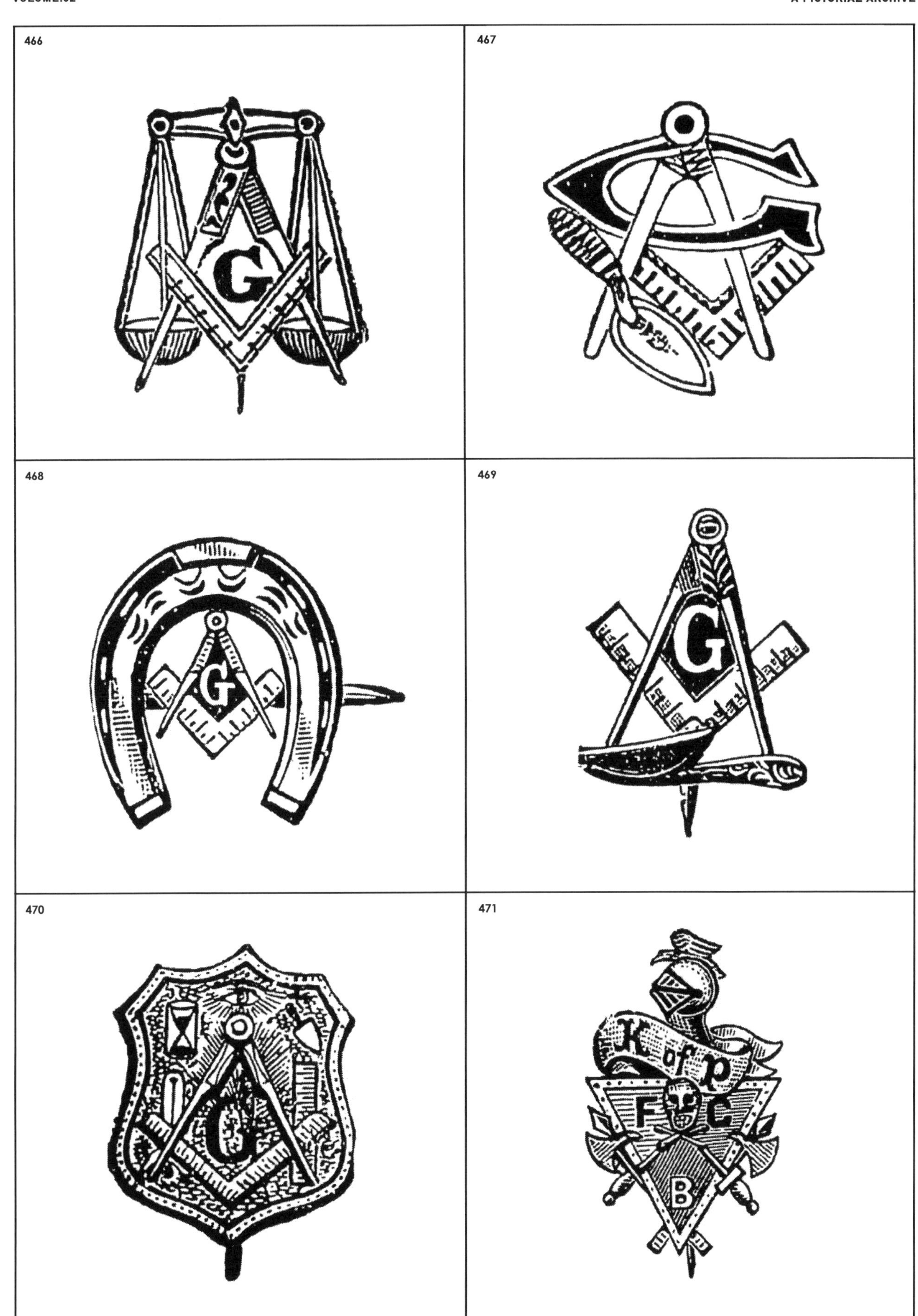
466
G
467
468
G
469
G
470
G
471
K of P
F C
B

472

473

474

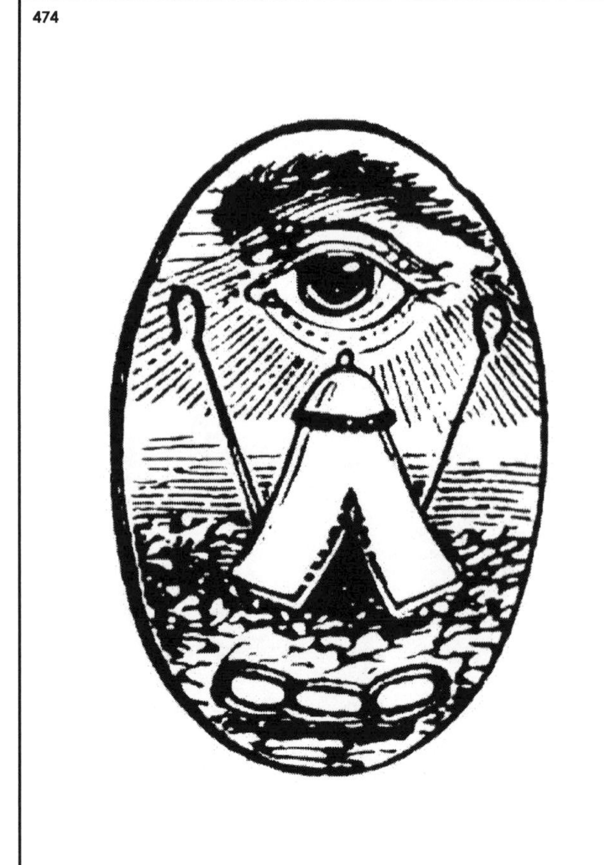

475

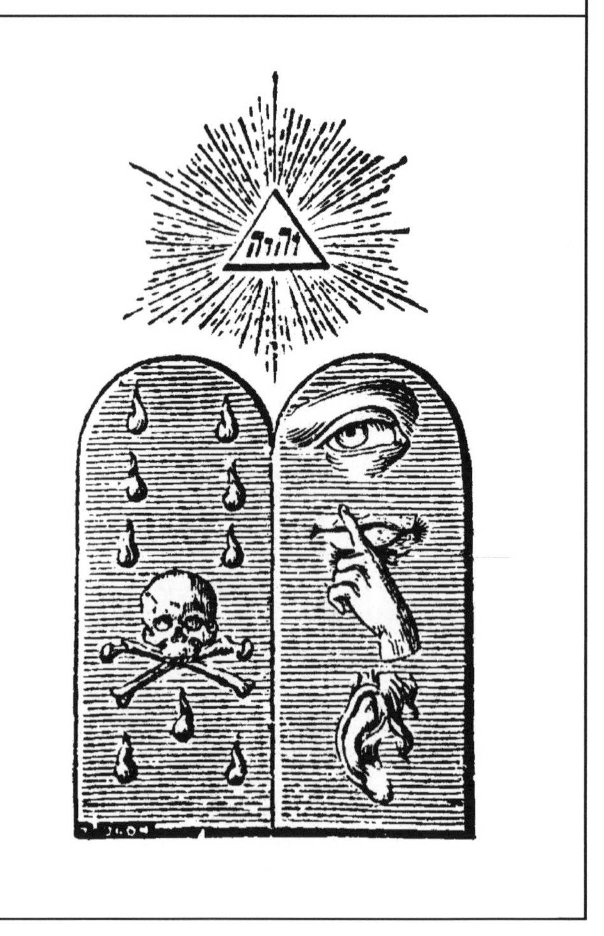

476

477

478

479

480

481

482

483

484

485

486

487

488

489

490

491

492

493
494
495
496
497
PERSEVERANTER
498
499

500
VIVITVR INGENIO CÆTERA MORTIS ERVT
501
PAVLATIM NON IMPETV
502
CŒCUS NIL LUCE IUVATUR
503
UTCUNQUE
504
PAR SIT FORTUNA LABORI.
505
BONA FIDE

506
BELLA IN VISTA DENTRO TRISTA.
507
VIVE MEMOR LETHI FUGIT HORA.
508
VIS NESCIA VINCI
509
INDIGNUM FORTUNA FOVET.
510
ABRUMPAM.
511
HINC DOLOR INDE FUGA.

512
FESTINATE DECURRERE.
513
NUSQUAM TUTA FIDES.
514
IN MANU DEI COR REGIS.
515
VIRTUS INEXPUGNABILIS.
516
LABORE ET CONSTANTIA.
517
VIRTUTE DUCE COMITE FORTUNA

518
HODIE MIHI CRAS TIBI.
519
MEMENTO MORI
520
IN SE SUA PER UESTIGIA UOLUITUR.
521
CONCORDIA INSUPERABILIS.
522
RERUM SAPIENTIA CUSTOS.
523
DISCITE IUSTITIAM.

VINTAGE LOGO DESIGN INSPIRATION COMPENDIUM

530
IXION
531
532
533
534
535

536
PRO ME SI MEREOR IN ME
537
FIDUCIA CONCORS
538
PER ANGUSTA AD AUGUSTA.
539
NE QUID NIMIS
540
VARIUM ET MUTABILE SEMPER
541
SIC SPECTANDA FIDES

542
FUROR FIT LÆSA SÆPIUS PATIENTIA
543
ASTRA DEUS REGIT
544
FERIO
545
QUOCUNQUE FERAR
Cubus
546
547
HODIE SIC VERTITUR ORBIS

548
IN MANU DOMINI. OMNES SUNT FINES TERRÆ.
549
NON INFERIORA SECUTUS.
550
OMNIS VICTORIA A DOMINO.
551
INSPERATA FLORUIT.
552
REDIBO PLENIOR.
553
VIRTUS UNITA FORTIOR.

554
FORTUNA. UT LUNA.
555
PAUPERTATE PREMOR SUBLEUOR INGENIO.
556
CONCEDO NULLI.
557
VERITAS PREMITUR NON OPPRIMITUR.
558
NON EST MORTALE QUOD OPTO.
ΓΑΝΥΜΗΔΗΣ.
559
NULLA DIES SINE LINEA.

560
PRO LEGE ET PRO GREGE.
561
TRANSITUS CELER EST ET AVOLAMUS
562
PRUDENTE SIMPLICITATE.
563
IN SPE ET LABORE TRANSIGO VITAM.
564
NON DORMIT QUI CUSTODIT.
EPIS COP.
565
NOLI ALTUM SAPERE.

566
A. FAC ET SPERA
567
A. NON SINE CAVSA
568
VIRTVS LORICA FIDELIS
569
DONEC TOTVM IMPLEAT ORBE
570
AVT MORS AVT VITA DECORA
571
VICTRIX FORTVNAE SAPIENTIA

572
TRIBVLATIO DITAT
573
574
RECTO CVRSV
575
ΑΙΩΝΙΟΝ ΚΑΙ ΠΡΟΣΚΑΙΡΟΝ
576
IN VIRTVTE ET FORTVNA
577
SVVM CVIQVE TRIBVE

578
ADVERSIS CLARIVS ARDET
579
GLORIA MVNDI SIC TRANSIT
580
MANET IMMVTABILE FATVM
581
DETERIVS FORMIDO
582
COR RECTV INQVIRIT SCIENTIĀ
ΔΙΑ
ΘΗΚΗ
583
ΕΚ ΠΟΝΟΥ ΚΛΕΟΣ

584
EX BELLO PAX
585
VIRTVTI FORTVNA COMES
586
TAMEN DISCAM
587
OMNIA MEA MECVM PORTO
588
HVMANA FVMVS
589
FIDE SED CVI VIDE

590
AMOR DOCET MUSICAM
591
STUDIO ET VIGILANTIA
592
SACRIFICIUM DEO COR CONTRIBULATUM
593
CONIUNCTIS VOTIS
594
FATO PRUDENTIA MAIOR
595
IN SILENTIO ET SPE

596
TVTIVS VT POSSIT FIGI
597
QVI ME ALIT ME EXTINGVIT
598
CONSENSV POPVLI REGNVM SVBSISTIT
599
DISCITE IVSTICIAM
600
INGENII LARGITOR VENTER
601
NEQVEO COMPESCERE MVLTOS

602
603
604
605
606
607

608
EX VTROQVE CÆSAR
609
SAPIENS DOMINABITVR ASTRIS
610
NON VNO STERNITVR ICTV
611
CONSEQVITVR QVODCVNQ PETIT
612
DVM EXTENDAR
613
DVM NVTRIO CONSVMOR

VINTAGE LOGO DESIGN INSPIRATION COMPENDIUM

620

VINTAGE LOGO DESIGN INSPIRATION COMPENDIUM

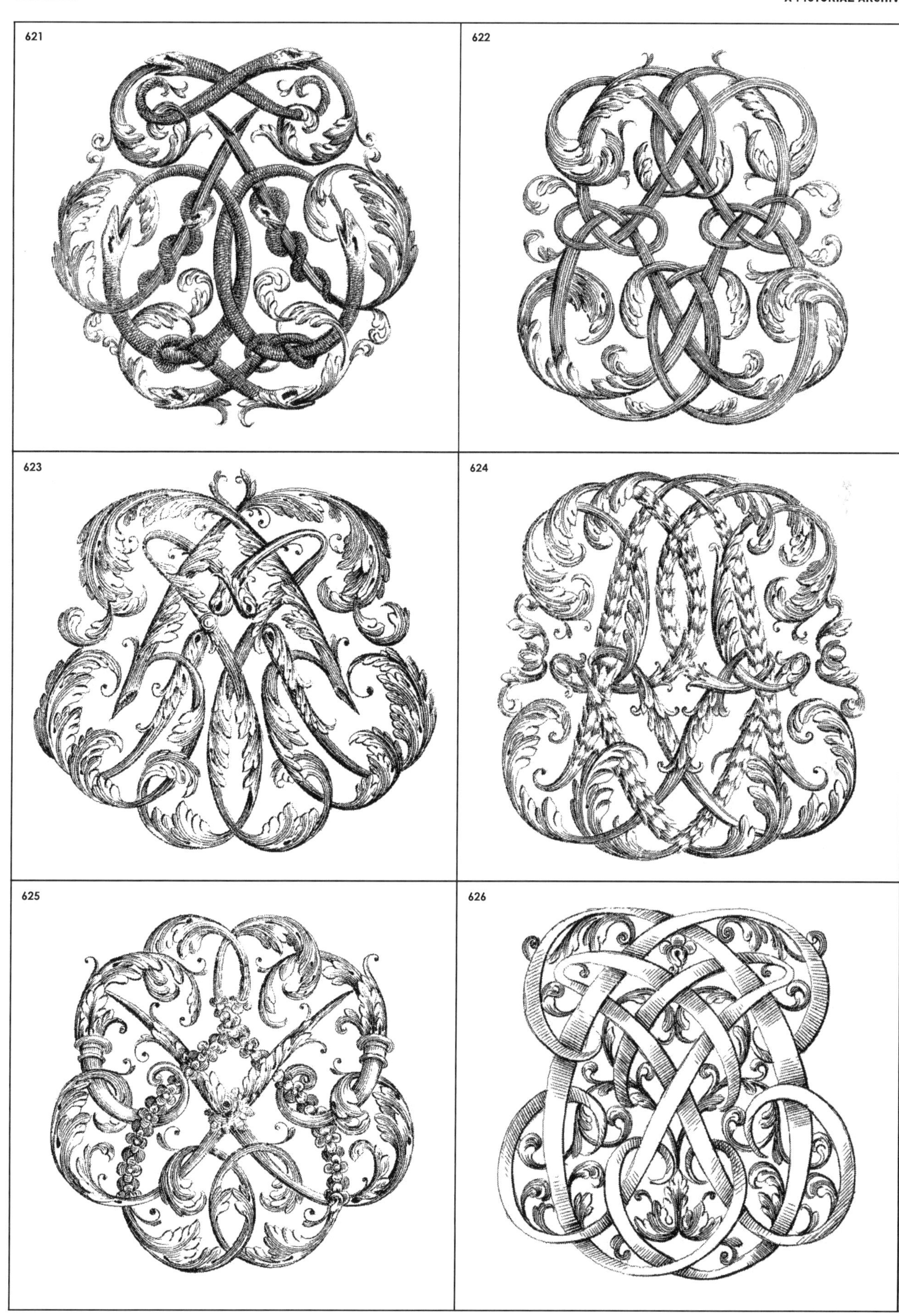
621
622
623
624
625
626

627

628

629

630

631

632

633

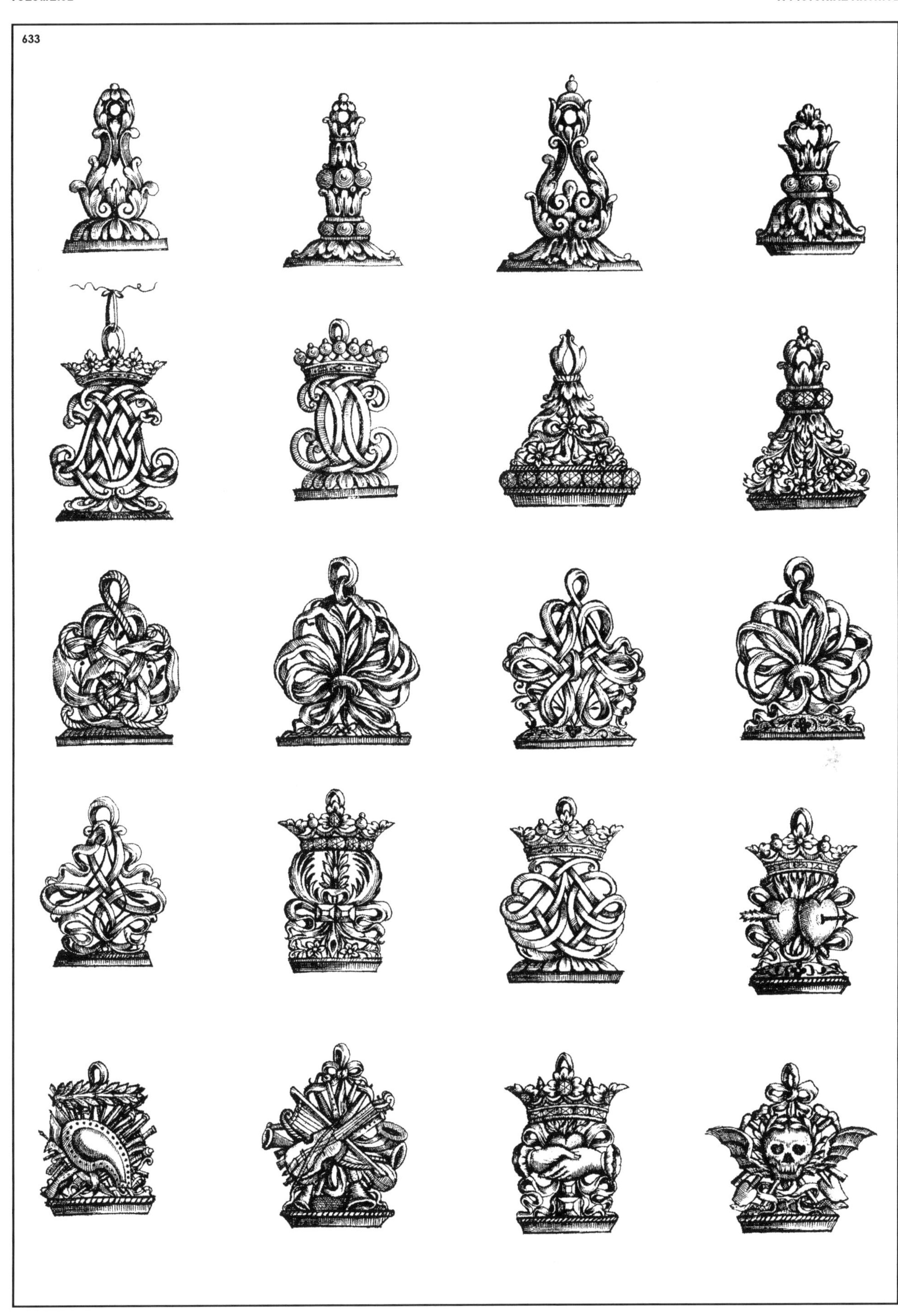

634

635

636

637

638

639

640

641

642

643

644

645

646

647

648

649

650

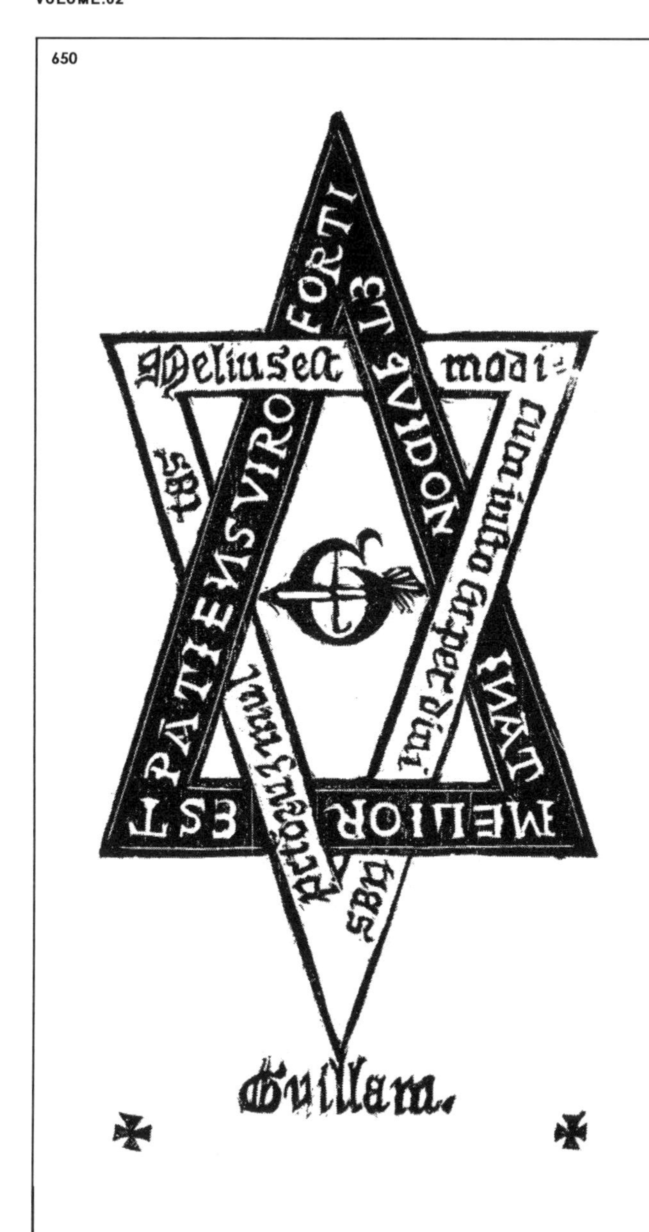

651

652

653

654

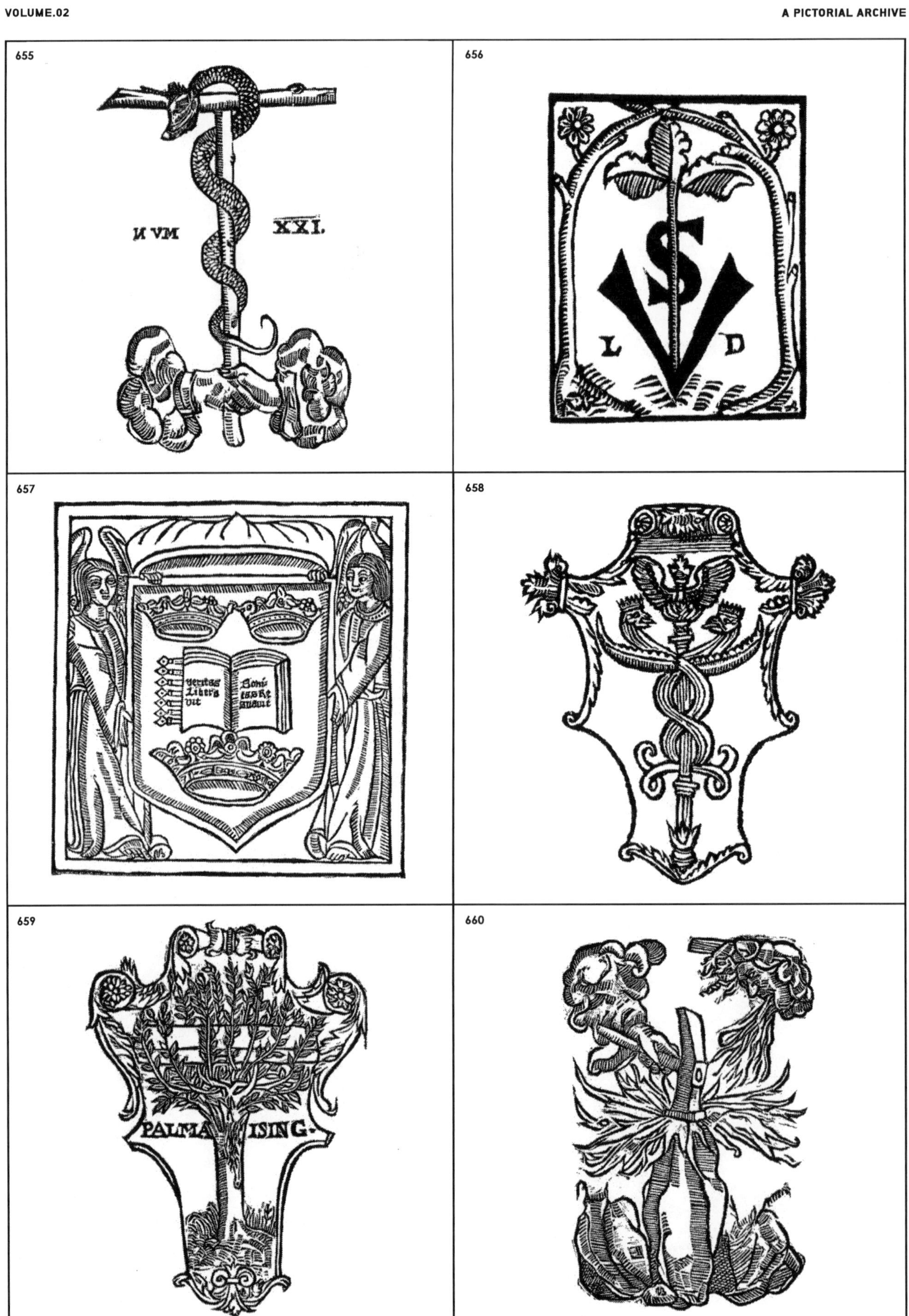
655
XXI.
656
S
L D
657
658
659
PALMA ISING.
660

661

662

663

664

665

666

667

668

669

670

671

672

673

674

675

676

677

678

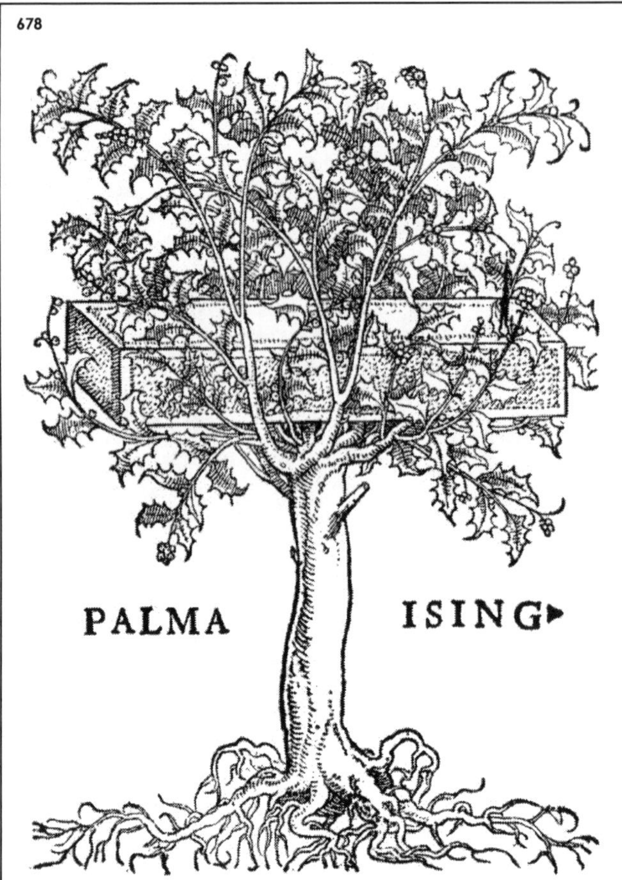

679

680

681

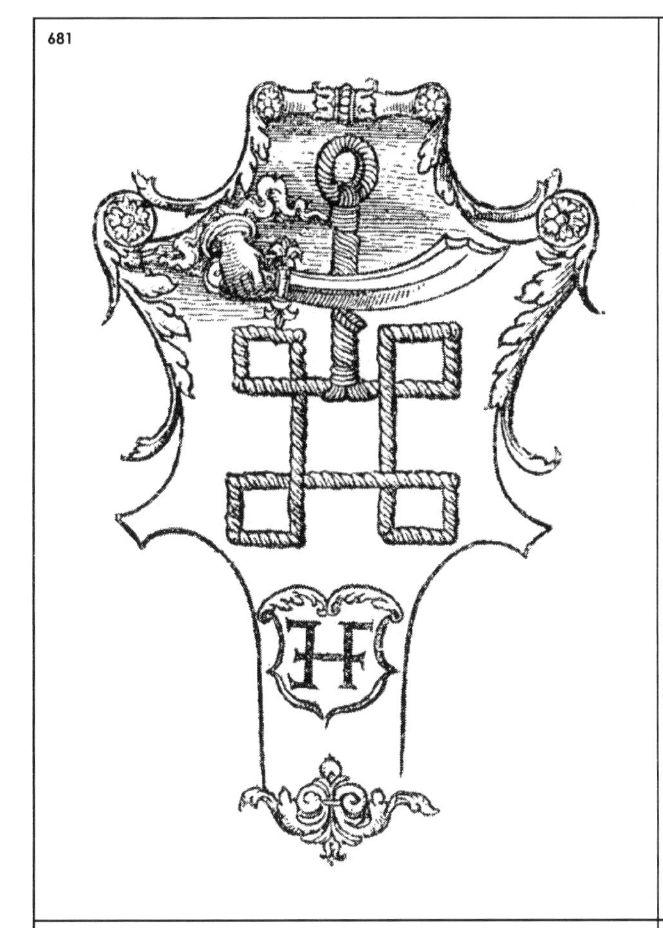

682

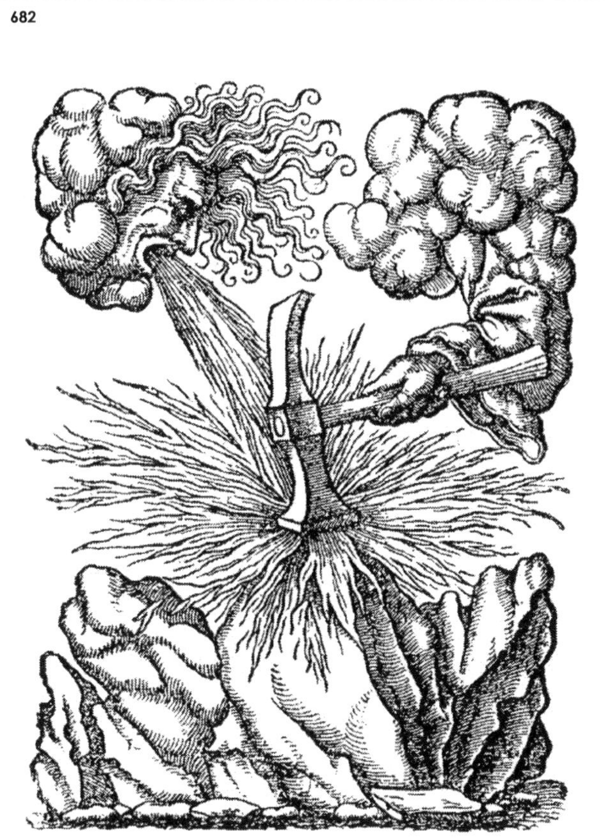

683

684

685

686

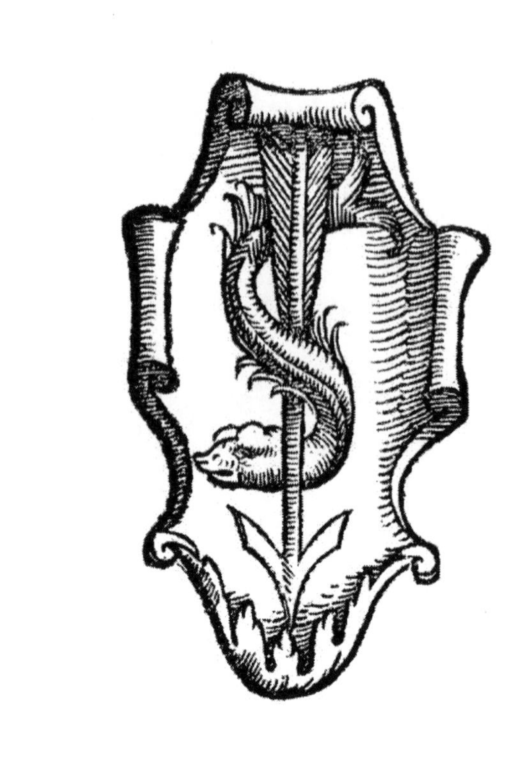

687

688

689

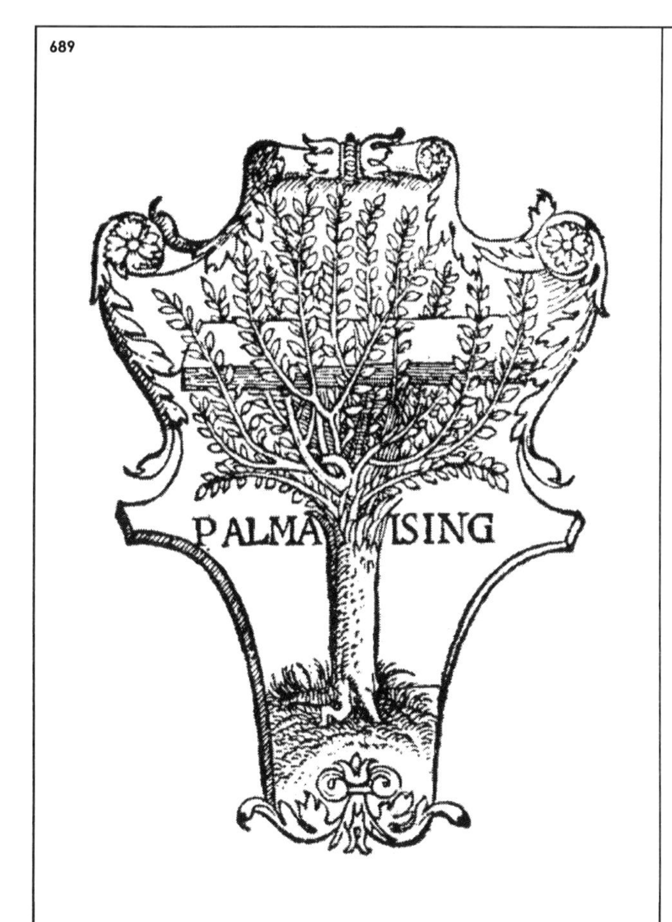

690

691

692

693

694

695

696

697

698

699

700

701

702

703

704
TORRENTIA
CONCVTIVNT SVMMAS
FVLGVRA QVERCVS.
705
IVST
I
TIA
DOMINI
PENDEMVS
OMNES
STATERA
IN
706
707
ENTIERE
COEVR
A FOY
708
FINIS CORONAT OPVS
709

710
ΛΟΓΩ ΕΡΓΩ
ΚΑΙ
711
RATIO MOVET ET REGIT ORBEM
712
713
ΦΡΑΔΗΝ
ΑΝΑΙΡΕΙ
ΛΟΤΟΣ
714
AD AMVSSIM DOLO,
ATQVE PERPOLIO,
SCABRA, ET IMPOLITA
715
SINE
FRAVDE.

716

717

718

719

720

721

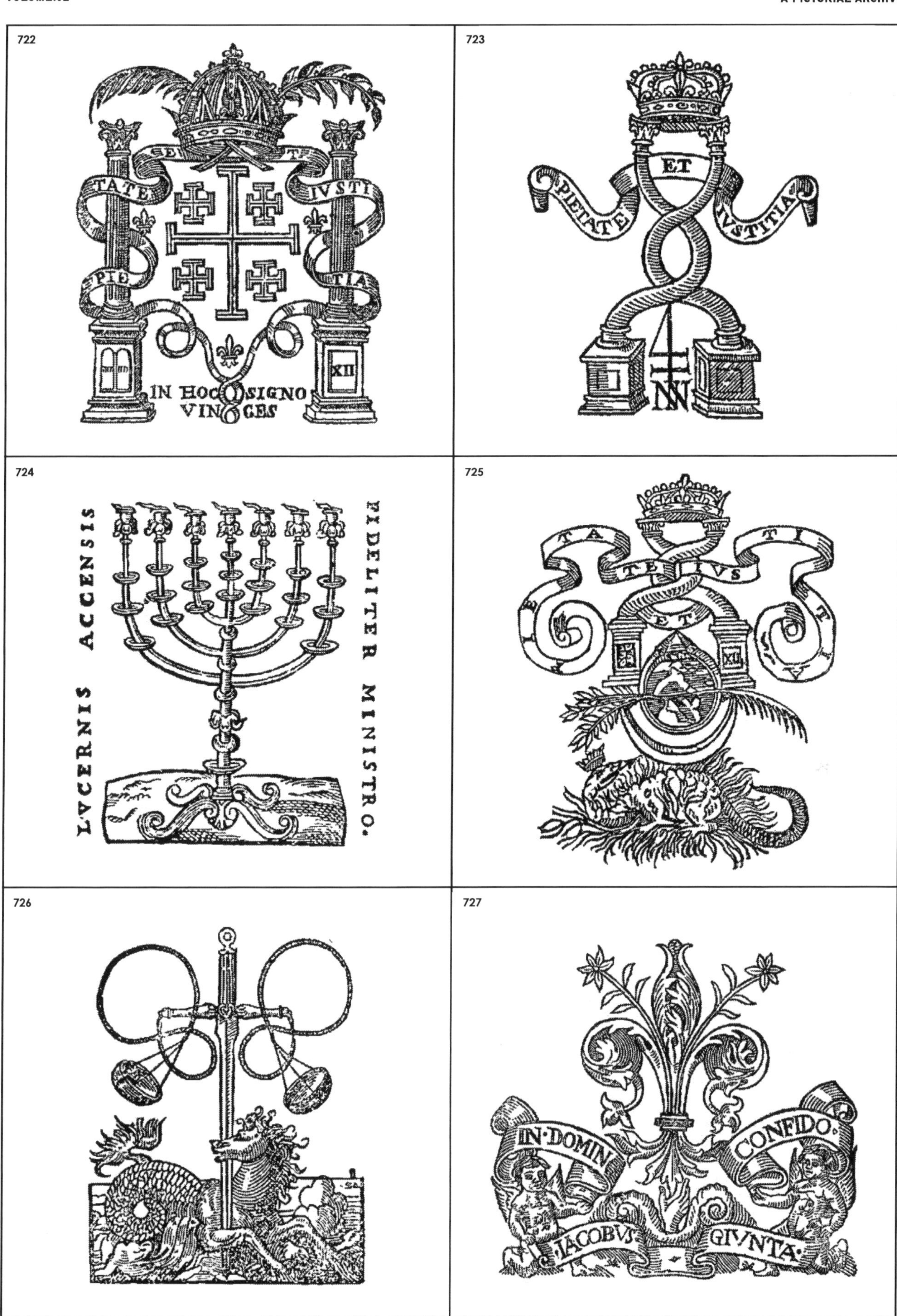
722
IN HOC SIGNO
723
PIETATE
ET
IVSTITIA
724
LVCERNIS ACCENSIS
FIDELITER MINISTRO.
725
726
727
IN·DOMIN
CONFIDO·
IACOBVS
GIVNTA·

728
729
730
SATIS QVERCVS.
731
VIGILANTI
732
IN
CVMBERE
EQVIS
FAMAE
HDG
733
IEHAN
HER
VER

734
IMBVTA RECENS SERVABIT ODOREM
735
736
FIDES IMPETRAT
QVOD LEX IMPERAT.
737
TEM PVS.
VIRTVS,SOLA ACIEM
RETVNDIT ISTAM
738
AL DVS
739
LABORE ET CONSTANTIA

740

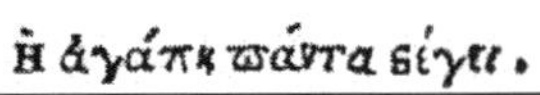

741

742

743

744

745

746

747

VINTAGE LOGO DESIGN INSPIRATION COMPENDIUM

754
755
LABORE ET CONSTANTIA
756
757
HANC
ACIEM
TEM
PVS
SOLA
RETVNDIT
VIR
TVS
758
EX TEMPORE
PRVDENTIA
759
NE LA MORT,
NE LE VENIN.

760

761

762

763

TANGIT MONTES

ET FVMIGANT.

764

765

766

767

768

769

VINTAGE LOGO DESIGN INSPIRATION COMPENDIUM

776

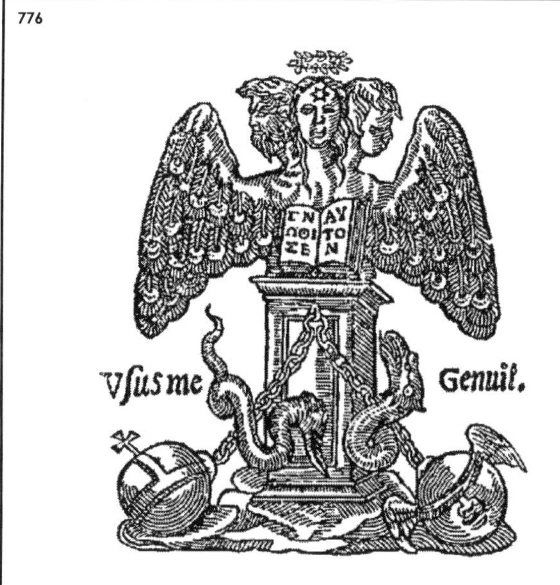

777

778

779

780

781

782

783

784

785

786

787

788

Οὕτως ἡδονῶν ἀπέχου τῶν ὀλεθρίων.

Sic perniciosis voluptatibus abstine.

789

HANC ACIEM SOLA RETVNDIT VIRTVS &c.
TEM PVS.

790

IN VNGVI GALLINA 1541

791

MATVRA.

792

793

794

795

796

797

798

799

800

801

802

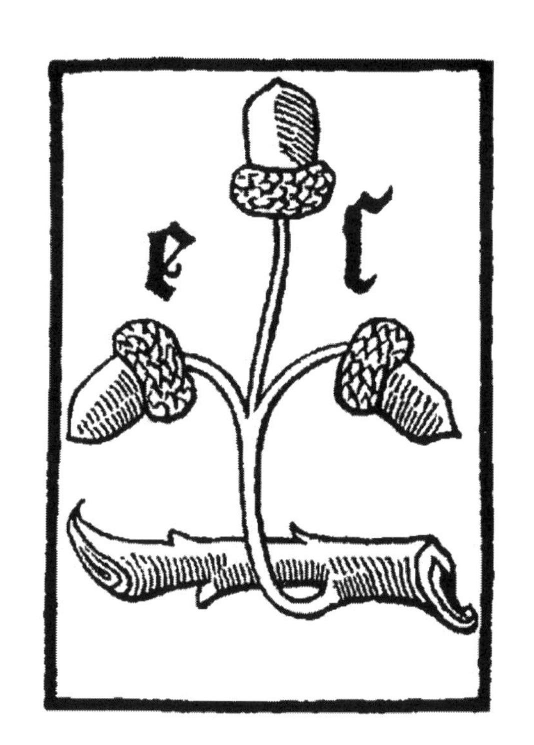

803

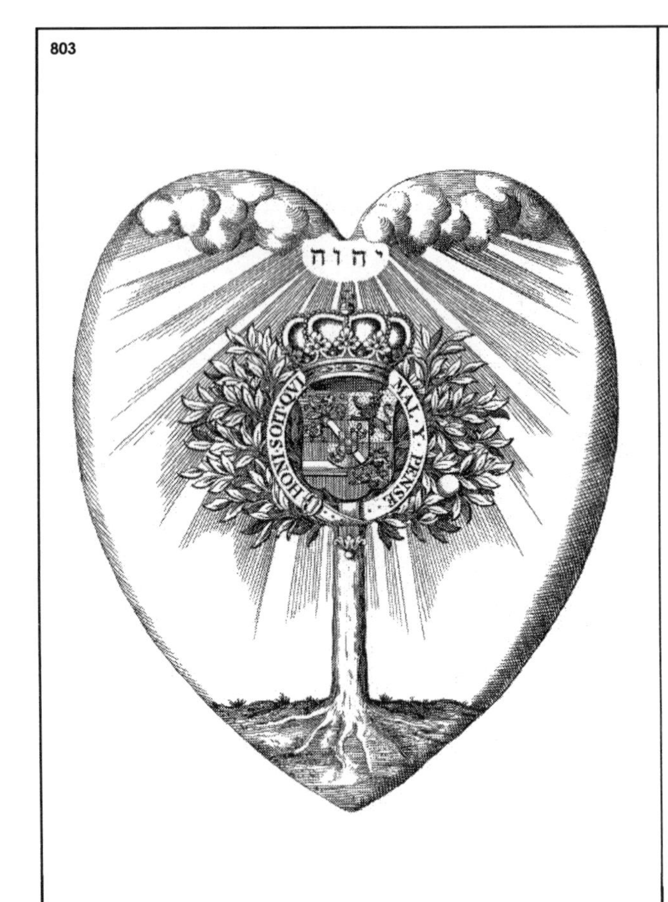

804

805

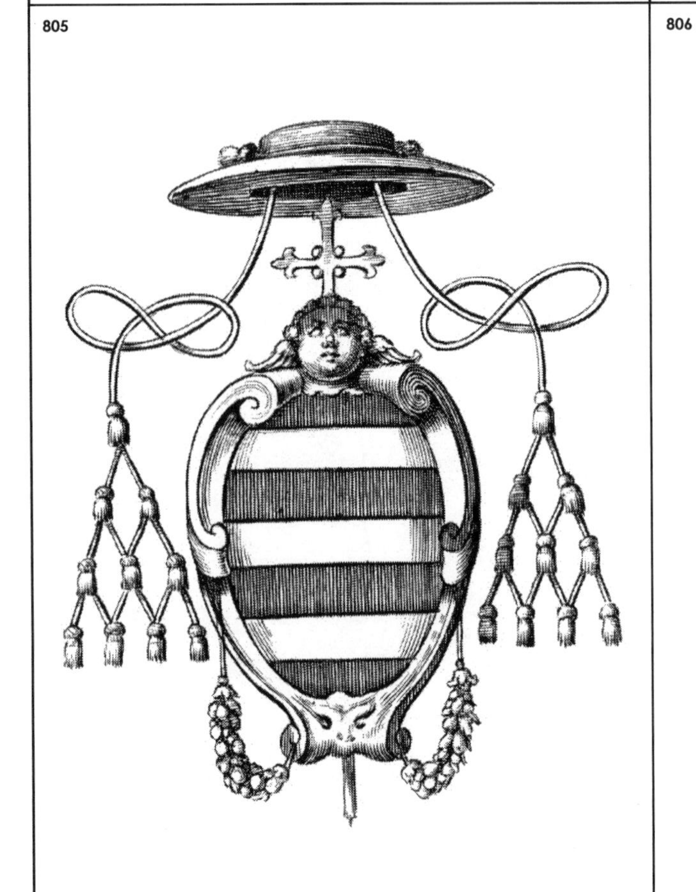

806

807

808

809

810

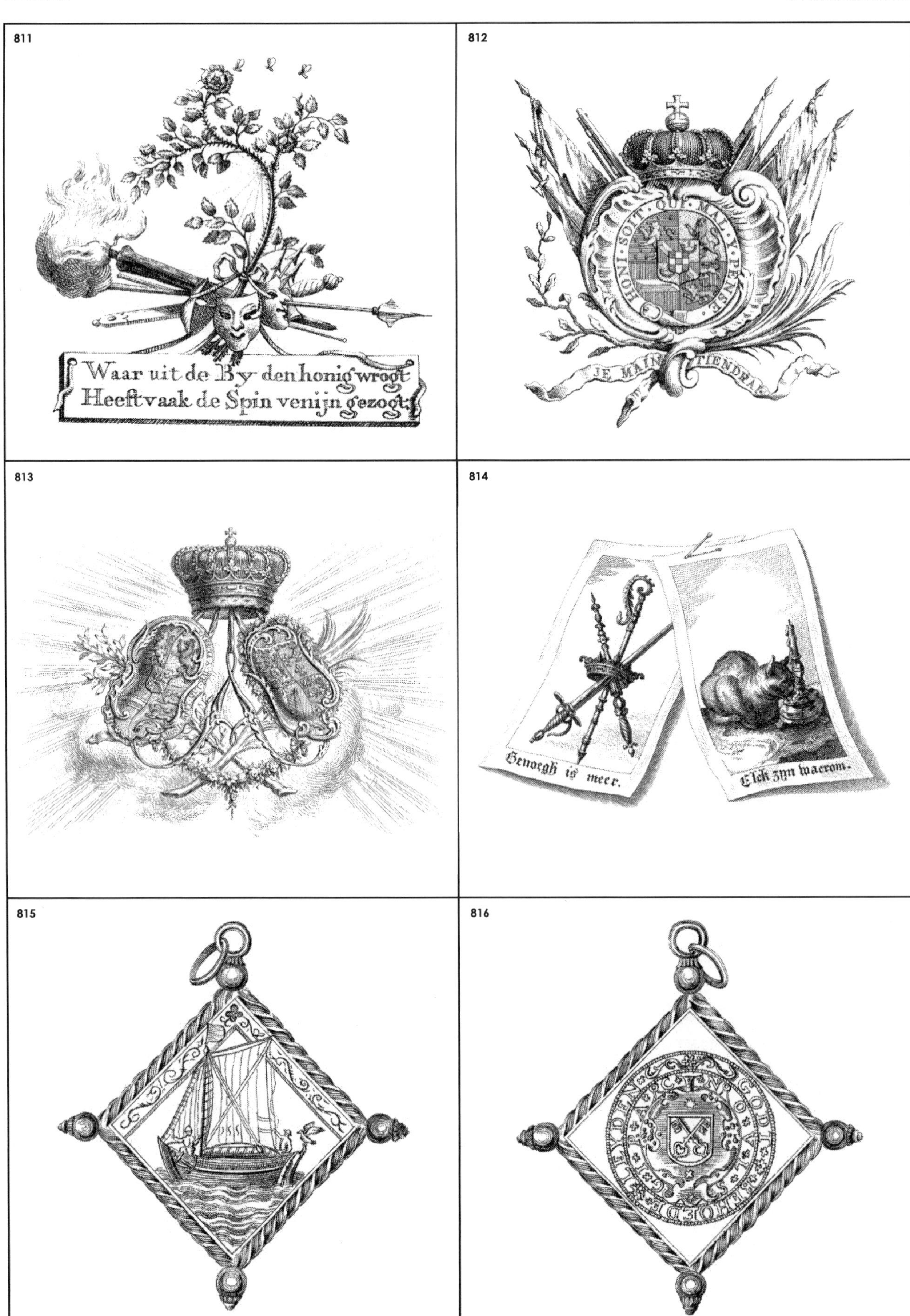
811
Waar uit de By den honig wrogt
Heeft vaak de Spin venijn gezogt
812
HONI SOIT QUI MAL Y PENSE
JE MAIN TIENDRAI
813
814
Genoegh is meer.
Elck zyn waerom.
815
816

817

818

819

820

821

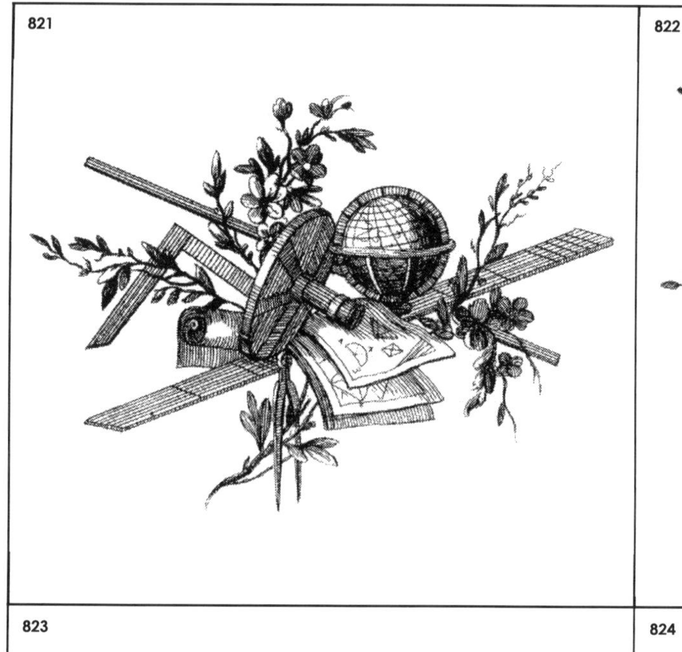

822

823

824

825

826
I R
HONI SOIT QVI MAL Y PENSE
827
REX ET SACERDOS DEI
828
829
NVLLVM BONVM INREMVNERATVM
830
C P
ICH DIEN
831
VNICA ETERNA AL MONDO

832

833

834

835

836

837

838
HONI SOIT QVI MAL Y PENSE
839
PATRIÆ ET DEO ET
840
HONI SOIT QVI MAL Y PENSE
841
QVEL CHE DRITTO DA IL CIEL TORCER NON PVOSSI
842
HONI SOIT QVI MAL Y PENSE
843
NON MANCA AL FIN SE BEN TARDA A VENIRE.

844
HONI SOIT QUI MAL Y PENSE
845
AVTHOREM. INVIDIA SVVM TORQVET
846
HONI SOIT QUI MAL Y PENSE
847
IMMOBILE CANDIDA
848
HONI SOIT QUI MAL Y PENSE
849
IN VTRAQVE PERFECTVS

850
851
RELIGIO VNVM COR VNVS DEVS VNA
852
853
NOS QVIS CONTRA
854
855
DODORE IL MONDO E D'ACVTEZZA IL CIELO

856
857
858
859
INSPEXIT SERO IVPITER DIPHTHERAM
860
861
DIVINVM VNVM ET ALTERVM

862
863
864
865
866
867

868
869
HONI SOIT QVI MAL Y PENSE
870
ICH DIEN
871
872
873

874
875
876
HONY SOIT QVI MALY PENSE
877
878
SPEM FORTUNA ALIT
879
DAVID DOMINVS LYNDESAY DE BALCARRES
ASTRA
CASTRA
NVMEN
LVMEN
MVNIMEN

880
FEAR GOD AND FEAR NOUGHT.
881
INGENUAS SUSPICIT ARTES
882
UNG DIEU
UNG ROY
883
CONSILIO
ANIMIS
IOANNES METELLANUS
LAUDERIÆ COMES
884
SA VERTU MA TIRE
885

886
887
MENS
CUIUSQUE IS EST
QUISQUE
888
889
HONI·SOIT·QUI·MAL·Y·PENSE
VIRTUTE·NON·VERBIS
890
891

892
MANUSCRIPT.
BIBLIOTHECA
SLOANEIANA.
893
894
895
DIEV
DEFENDE LE
DROICT
896
897

898
HONI SOIT QUI MAL Y PENSE
DIEU ET MON DROIT
899
AVGVSTA
VINCENTI
900
Honi soit mal y pense
901
902
903
TRIA JUNCTA IN UNO
NEC PRECE NEC PRETIO

904
AGE QUOD AGIS
905
NON EST MORTALE QVOD OPTO
SEMPER EADEM
VIENDRA
NE VILE
BON TEMPS
906
CAVENDO
TUTUS
907
908
COR VNV VIA VNA
909

910
DIEV ET MON DROIT
911
FIDE LITATE ET SAGACI TATE
H C
912
FIEL PERO DESDICHADO
913
DIEU DEFEND LE DROIT
914
915
R D

916
E
P
IHC·DIEN
917
SIC·DONEC
918
919
SOIT·QUI
MAL·Y·
PENSE
HONI
920
921
DIEU
ET·MON
DROIT

922
SOIT·QUI·MAL
DIEU·ET
MON
DROIT
923
III
924
VIRTUTE·ET·FIDE
925
HONORABO HONORANTES : ME :
926
927

928
929
930
931
932
933

934
935
936
937
938
939

940
941
942
943
944
945

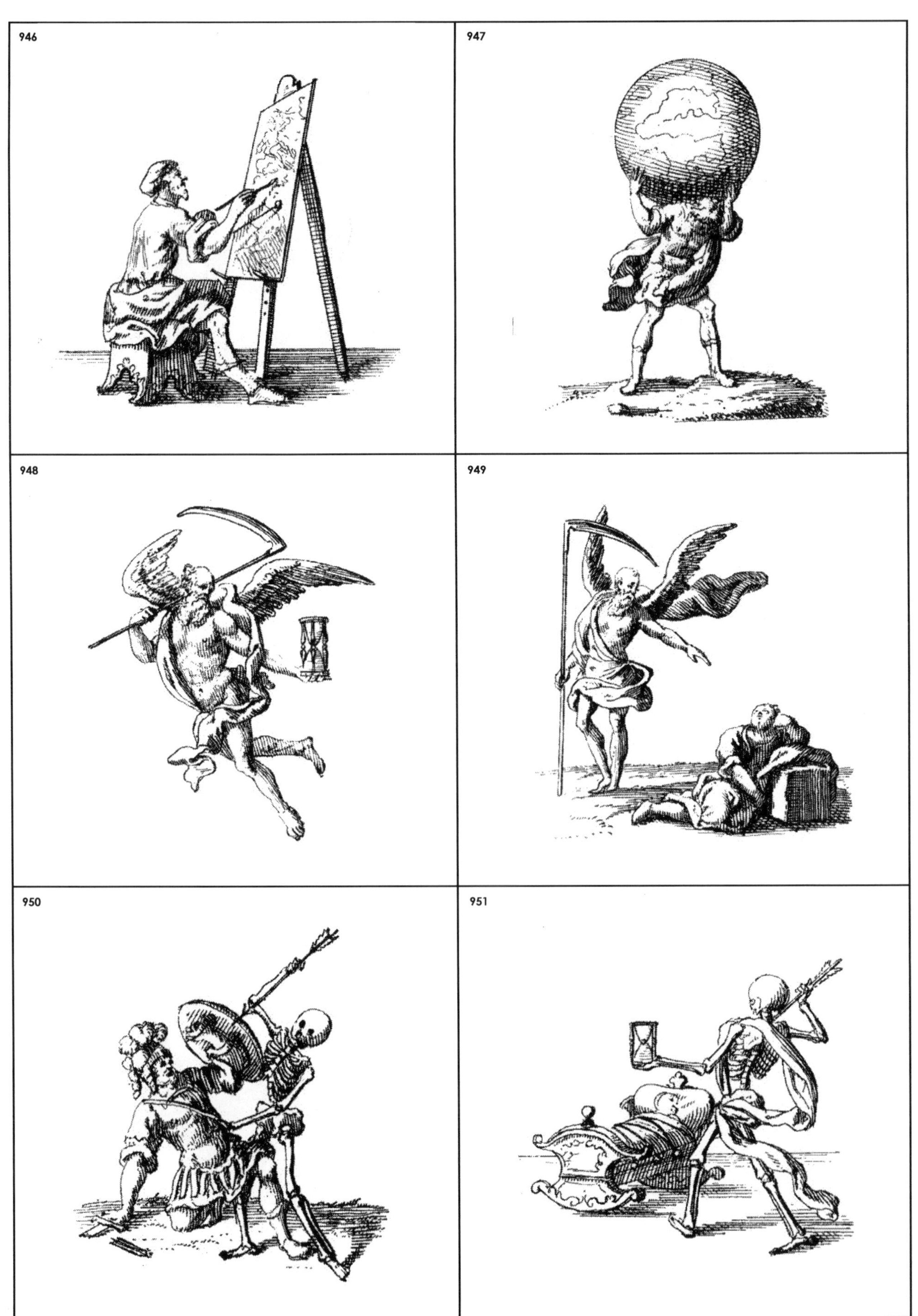
946
947
948
949
950
951

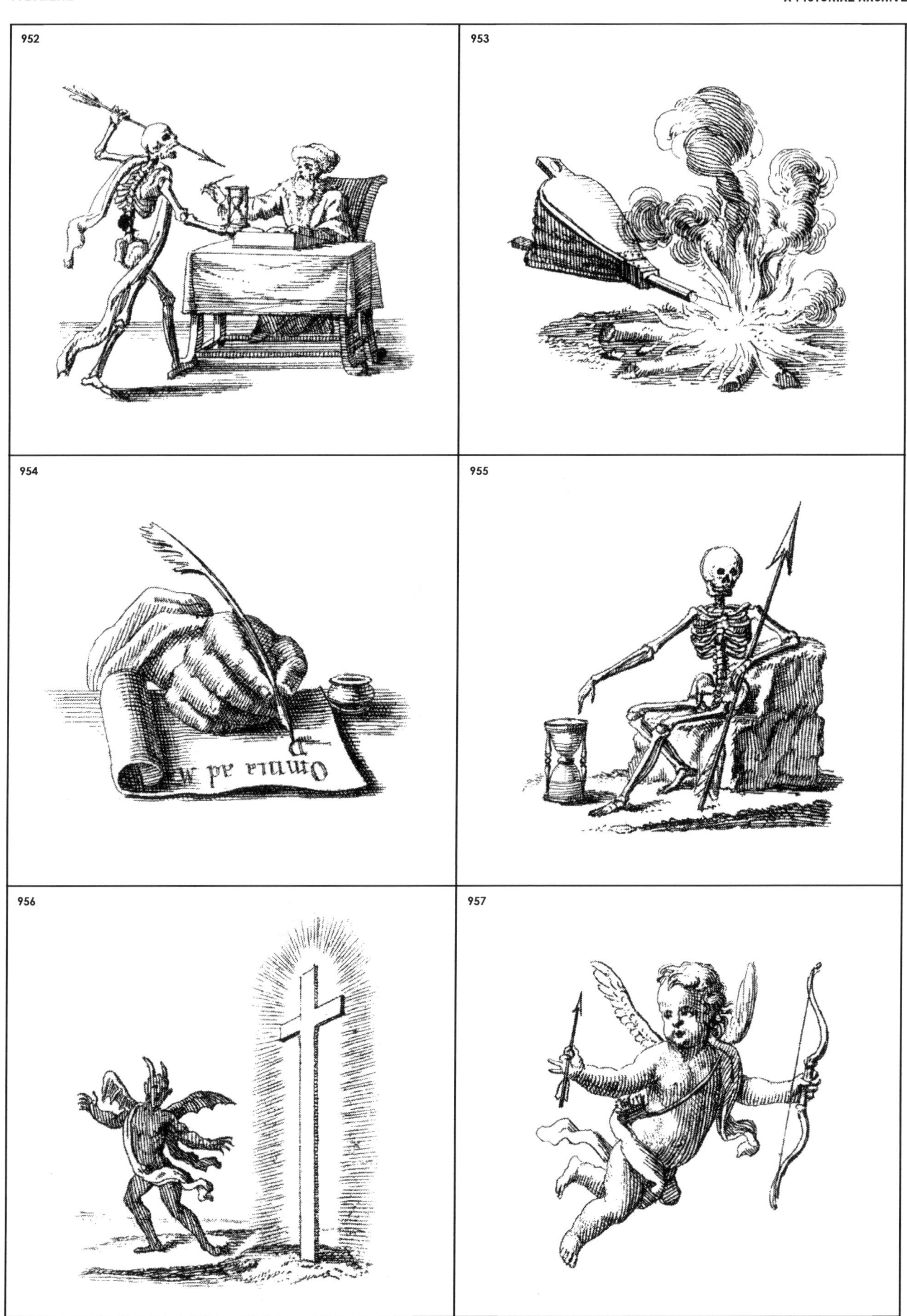
952
953
954
955
956
957

958
959
960
961
962
963
MDCLXX

964
965
966
967
968
969

970
971
972
973
974
975

976
977
978
979
980
981

982
983
984
985
986
987

VINTAGE LOGO DESIGN INSPIRATION COMPENDIUM

LEARN MORE

At Vault Editions, our mission is to create the world's most diverse and comprehensive collection of image archives available for artists, designers and curious minds. If you have enjoyed this book, you can find more of our titles available at vaulteditions.com.

REVIEW THIS BOOK

As a small, family-owned independent publisher, reviews help spread the word about our work. We would be incredibly grateful if you could leave an honest review of this title wherever you purchased this book.

JOIN OUR COMMUNITY

Are you a creative and curious individual? If so, you will love our community on Instagram. Every day we share bizarre and beautiful artwork ranging from 17th and 18th-century natural history and scientific illustration, to mythical beasts, ornamental designs, anatomical illustration and more. Join our community of 100K+ people today—search @vault_editions on Instagram.

DOWNLOAD YOUR FILES

STEP ONE

Enter the following web address in your web browser on a desktop computer.

www.vaulteditions.com/vlict

STEP TWO

Enter the following unique password to access the download page:

vlict239472cvb

STEP THREE

Follow the prompts to access your high-resolution files.

TECHNICAL ASSISTANCE

For all technical assistance, please email: info@vaulteditions.com

Made in the USA
Las Vegas, NV
11 September 2023